Chapter 1 Losing a loved one

Sometimes life can be so difficult especially when you about to lose a loved one. Hi, my name is Lauren first off let me tell you what happen to me when I was little and then I will continue sharing my personal story with you. When I was little, I was lying in bed I remember, and I was wide awake with my Barney the dinosaur in one hand and my teddy bear in the other. Suddenly, I was lifted. You may think it was a dream, but it was not. It could have been the wind, but it was not. What it was an angel that lifted me from my bed where the window was.

The first loved one I lost is my Papa. One day it started back in November of 2017. That I found out that my Papa was diagnosed with stage 4 lung cancer and the doctor said he only had a few months to live. Now that is when losing a loved one hurt me most. But however, the loved one you lose will always be in your heart. However, the pain of losing a loved one will never heal. Now God and Jesus are in control with the loved one you had lost. What I can tell you that special loved one you had lost. You will see again just not right away. Right now, that special loved one you had lost will be in your dreams and always inside your heart.

Some ways it helps me is I always remember the good times. But at times I still get emotional everyone has their days. However, losing that love one can be difficult. Also, I can tell you losing a loved one never is easy. Losing a pet or a human. One advice I can give you is only remembering the good times. Try not to remember the tough times. Here is why if you remember the tough times, it will just make you more depressed.

Now let me tell you about the pet that I had growing up her name was Magee Beeb, and she was a beagle. She loved to play and run around. Her birthday was December 30th. Now I cannot remember the exact year she was born. In May 2012 we had to put her down. she was old. However, she did have a tumor on her tail and the best thing we could do is putting her down. She went to heaven where God and Jesus are. The next loved one we lost is Cooper and he was a white Maltese and a rescue. Also, he had a lot of nicknames. His actual name was JoJo, but our family changed it to Cooper he had a bad life. But then he had a great life when he came to us. He passed away in January 2020. Again, not only he was old, but he also had cancer. He had a lot of anxiety and he always like to beat to his own drum. Lastly, we lost our beloved first golden retriever Polly Jane also known as Polly love and she had a lot of nicknames that I will state in here. Which is Polly love, Polygon, Paw Paws and Polly Wally doodle all day and sometimes we say does Polly want a cracker. She was terrified of thunder, blow dryers water, and other loud noises like fireworks. Her Birthday is June 29th and she passed not only she was getting old, but she had some cancer as well. She passed away May 2022. She was a great dog she loved everyone including her toys. However, I produced a special song for her. "Polly love Polly love she makes everyone smile at least for a while. She also liked going on walks, getting treats, and going on car rides. Those were a little bit about the pets I have lost my beloved pets. Now let me tell you about some very wonderful humans I had lost recently. The first one is my Great Grandma which is my Papa's mom. To me Papa is just another name for grandpa. Also, that was my mom's dad. Anyways, my Great Grandma passed on April 23rd, 2022. She was just a beautiful lady. She was a great baker and was so loved by many. She had a kind heart and one of her nicknames we called her was Gidley. Lastly, we lost my grandpa which is my dad's dad. My grandpa passed on August 22nd, 2022. He was a veteran of the U.S. Army. He also worked for a pipeline, He also enjoyed woodworking and making wooden bowls which was sold all over the world. He liked Basketball and Football, and he also had a passion for Genealogy. Now back to my Papa and the things that he liked. He liked riding on motorcycles, He was a welder, and he will never stop working and I always called him my Papa Billy. Throughout the chapters there will be more about this.

Losing a loved one the pain will never go away. You will always have a special memory with the pet or human you had lost. But I can tell you this you will always have them with you in your hearts and by looking up in the sky. You can picture them with you wherever you go. It is okay to cry it out all the time or occasionally. At times I still get emotional. Everyone has their days and losing that loved one can be difficult for sure. Like I said even though they are no longer here on earth with us. They always hold a special place inside of your heart. We all had lost that one special pet or human in our lifetime. But we all have different feelings on how to express losing a loved one.

It may be sadness which you may feel upset or angry and frustrated. But again, that is okay because no one is perfect. But I know that you have people to talk to about losing a loved one. All you must do is to learn how to overcome it. Just by hearing other people stories of the loved ones they lost. Will help you so much. However, sometimes I know you want to keep things to yourself. Now I am not saying it is not a dreadful thing. It is not a terrible thing at all. Sometimes you just must express your feelings by showing it. Basically, feeling others pain will help as well. We are all in the same boat. You just must have strength and know that they had a great life. Now they are with our savior and for your life goes on. Also, they will be happy whatever you do. Go keep on doing what you are doing and take every chance you can get. Somedays you will have reminders pop up and that is okay as well. Losing a loved one is one of the toughest things in life. Just remember they may be faraway. But however, they will never leave your side and they will always be in your heart. Also, if you look for signs like birds or find a dime on the ground or when the lights go out. What it means is that a loved one is near. Of course, sometimes you do remember the troubled times of losing a loved one. But remember the good times. They will always have a special place in your heart. One thing I like to do is look at the airplanes in the sky. Here is why because my Papa use to like flying in airplanes. Airplanes just helped me think of a special loved one I lost. Airplanes are just a calming feeling. Also, watching bird is too. That is the reason and just a great reminder that our loved ones just flying to heaven. That is what I like to do when it is light out. Now when it is dark out, I like to look at the moon and stars and picture the loved ones I have lost. Try not to remember the tough times. Just remember the good times and all the love and memories you share. You will see them again I promise you. However, just not right now. But you can see them in your dreams. What you need to do is go on and focused on your life. Also, know that they will be okay in heaven. You just got to know that they are safe with God and Jesus our savior.

Chapter 2 Faith Over Fear

Have you sometimes felt like you have faith and know your loved ones you about to lose will be okay. To tell you the truth it is the other way around. But it can be different for everybody. For me fear comes before faith. The reason is I am afraid of losing a pet or that special human at first. But once they go to heaven to be with our savior which is Jesus. What I know is that they are no longer in pain. Then I have faith for them and knowing that they are going to be okay. Sometimes I have this fear when they are about to be gone. Especially, if I do not get a chance to say goodbye and tears are just running down my cheeks. We all feel like that just not me but everyone. We just have various levels of expressing it. But what scared me the most is when somebody tells me that the loved one is on its way to heaven. What I thought that loved one had already passed and I did not get a chance to say goodbye. But you must be prepared and have the faith to know that loved one will be okay.

Faith means strength and to have faith. You need to have strength and know that loved one had may live a short or long life. Which is hard in away and I know that because I had experience it. However, I do know this fear is losing them and that they are not in your life no more. The faith is that you know that they are in a good place, and they do not have to suffer anymore. But you must have the faith to continue to live your life. None of us know that when our ticket is going to be pulled. That is why we need to take one day at a time and love much as we can here on earth in this world. Also, help as much as we can as well. The loved ones that we lost are in another world called heaven. Fear means scary losing them and feeling shaken and nervous. But faith means to shall not be shaken and to know your loved ones will be okay and know that you will be okay.

For me I do not like the word death that is my fear. This is the reason I want to replace the word death and use losing. When I use the word death it just scares me, and I always have nightmares. Same as they talk about cremated and buried in the ground is another thing scares me. This is another reason I do not use the word death I replace it with losing or passing. But I know you do not feel anything when you passed. You   must have faith to continue. Hope that who lived on earth have faith too. What I can say is that I know we all on various levels of faith and fear. The way that I see it is you must overcome it. Also, fear means afraid. Sometimes you feel afraid of passing or dying whatever word you prefer to use. We are all different and how we see things. Like I said we all have various levels. For a fact I know it is hard to talk about this. Just helping you to guide you and sharing my ideas of me being scared with fear and how I can overcome it with faith. Sometimes we got to talk about these things. Like some do not like to talk about this and that person is me.

My biggest fear is seeing someone else passed. Seeing my Papa passed does not want me to go to another funeral again. The reason is because I can see it in my own mind. However, I always think that person could have been me. Also, I still cannot get the image out of my head. But I do know that I need to put the work in to have faith to overcome it. Another thing is that you must put more work in and face fear. Even though it may be hard.

Yes, I also believe that fear can also lead stress in losing a loved one. We all are afraid but we all know it can be terrifying. But you also must look on the bright side. Now that bright side is faith. You must find the strength to continue.

Also, my parents gave me tips just act like they are sleeping. If you really must go to a funeral and just remember the good times you had with that special loved one. Even though the image may never go away in your mind. Between that is fear and faith. You just must take the good with the bad.

Chapter 3 Follow the Rainbow

There are two types of sides of rainbows. One side of the rainbow is earth, and the other side is heaven. This is how I imagine it. Even though I know they have this thing called rainbow bridge where your pets go. But this is different, and this is how I picture it.

The way that I see it is that one side is planet earth, and the other side is heaven where the loved ones we lost goes. What I told my golden retriever Polly before she passed. Is that I will see you on the other side of the rainbow. But just not right now I told her. What I am going to say is this. When I see a rainbow in the sky, I will look on the other side and picture the loved ones I lost. Also, you will be able to do the same and make sure that they are never forgotten.

The other side of the rainbow is where human and pets we have lost. When they are on the side of the rainbow, and this is what I am thinking. They are thinking about us. On the planet earth side as well. Every time when I see a rainbow, I like to have flashbacks of the loved ones I lost. Like I said before I hope you do the same thing. Try not to think about the tough times. Only try to think of the good times. You may break down and cry but that is okay.

Again, on the other side of the rainbow where our loved ones we have lost. Are doing the same thing. However, they are only doing it spiritually. It is like that song somewhere over the rainbow from the Wizard of Oz. This is what I can tell you somewhere on the other side of the rainbow is our loved ones and I know it is so far away. But I know that they are near inside in your hearts and every step of your journey. Loved ones that we lost will always be on the other side of the rainbow. Also, it is like you follow the rainbow and they are following your hearts at the same time. If you just give it a chance and believe. Then you will really know loved ones are near and they are finding their path to you. Just think of magical creatures as well. Like unicorns, butterflies, or a Leprechaun. Believe in those things that bring you luck that goes over the rainbow and birds as well.

Rainbows are also beautiful sign that our loved ones we have lost reminding us they are always with us. Another way I know rainbow are supposed to be happy and bright. But to tell you the truth there is also sadness involved. The reason it is because it is God creation. Also, it is where our loved ones are on the other side of the rainbow where heaven is. They will never ever leave us. If we cannot, see them right now. But one day I guarantee we will. However, for now they remain in our hearts. Until one day we cross the other side of the rainbow and meet again. But right now, they will always remain in our hearts.

Chapter 4 Finding the Light

Finding the light, it is like finding a shooting star. When the lights go off and it means it is time for our loved ones to go and it is very heartbreaking. But finding out they are in peace and now it is time for them to rest. To know that they lived their best life as they can. By knowing that they found the light to God and to our savior Jesus. You got to remember that they are safe now.

Now they are lighting up the sky and I know you are no longer gotten to see them. Only in your dreams and spiritually you can see them. But you know that there are always signs of your loved ones. Which are airplanes, sun, and clouds and throughout the chapters of this book I will be repeating a lot of things. You can always light up a candle and your loves one is near. But when the light goes out in the candle. What it means is that it is time for you to rest. Also, it is time for our loved ones to rest in heaven. But then you can see each other in your dreams.

When you see lighting bugs you can tell a loved one is near heaven. Also, when you find the light, it always led to darkness. Again, when your lights go out and it means it is time for your loved ones to get some rest in heaven. It also means you must get some rest on earth. Or less if you are somewhere where it is a different time frame. Let see what else oh or like when the power goes out at place. It also means a sign from your loved ones from heaven. To know that they are coming to say hi. Sometimes it is hard to believe but it is true. If you find the light and I believed you will find your loved ones from heaven through the darkness. What anyways how I see it. For a fact I know we all see things differently. However, it may mean you get to see it too unbelievably. We all do not see things the same way. What we all see is different views of it.

Also, if a light bulb burns out. Or if the light will not turn off. A loved one is still near heaven. It also can be opposite as well. When it gets dark your loved ones are with you. If the lights flicker on and off your loved ones are still nearby. If the light stays on, they can still be with you no matter what. We all have a way of thinking differently and that is okay. There are no wrong way or answer.

As I mentioned before this may sound scary. But when the lights go on and off. It also means your loved ones are coming to say hi from heaven. Also, if you see a shadow that it is not your own. It means that a loved one from heaven is coming to say hi. Another thing is when the sunlight comes in. When it is nice and bright outside. Also, when the sunset comes above it also remind you of heaven. Where our loved ones we lost are. Darkness led to light like a shooting star. If you see a shooting star in the sky it is a sign. You also can make a wish. Seeing a shooting star will be amazing but it really does not happen. Here is why I am saying if you see any star, it will really be a sign as well. Stars you can see every night. A shooting star not really. Sometimes however stars can shine bright as a diamond. Either way the light will shine bright. Even when you hear the wind a loved one is also nearby. Or you can leave footprints too. Sometimes it may sound shocking when you go to the beach and say those are not my footprints. You can think this way that it is also a sign that your loved one is near. Also, if you where your loved ones from heaven old clothing. It is also a sign. Like for an example I always like to wear my Papa's hat. Even though sometimes you do not like to be reminded. It may be true to you, or it may be false that it does not work out. You got to keep your light shining here on earth. Your loved one must keep shining wherever heaven is. But what I said before is that heaven is mystery. All I know is that it is far away. Your loved one will also be dancing for you. Sometimes I do hear voices. The voices are my loved ones I lost. Our loved ones from heaven will find us in the valley and on the mountains. On the beach our loved ones will be walking and standing with us from heaven as well. Sometimes you just must have the light follow you wherever you go. You just got to walk in the valley of death in darkness. Again, I really do not like using the word death. Keep your light shining and the loved one from heaven will keep their light shining as well. Also, just like a flashlight in the dark when that flashlight runs out of battery. It also means it is time for our loved ones to get some rest. Or they may want to stick around with us for a while. Your loved ones will always think of you from heaven. If you think of them too.

They will always believe in us if you always believed in them and never forget about your loved ones in heaven. You are never alone in life you still have your loved ones if they are here on earth with us or in heaven. However, you may ask questions about your loved one you lost and know that they will always be with you

Chapter 5 Are you Scared?

When it comes losing a loved one yes it can be scary and the question you got to asked yourself too. Are you scared? However, when that special loved one or pet that goes home to our savior. By knowing that they are scared as much as you are. The reason is because they do not want to leave earth or you. Got to know that none of us cannot live forever. Now my question is are you scared of a loved one leaving earth to go to heaven? Well, let me tell you I am terrified. Here is why when I lost my loved ones and how it affected me. For an example when I attend both of my Papa's and Grandpa funerals. However, I always have this weird feeling in my mind. Even though they are gone I can still see them breathing. For me that can be a scary thing. If even, I know that they are at peace. Now the second thing is that I do not really like to go to cemeteries. Every time I fear going and I always end up having nightmares. However, we all do see things differently. At the same time when I go to cemeteries a lot of emotions hit me. Not only I am scared but I am also sad. It is scary losing a loved one and everyone have various levels of emotions.

You will be alarmed after losing a loved one. However, that loved one will also be scared as well. Plus, they will be alarmed leaving planet earth. To go to this beautiful place called heaven. When you pass and go to heaven you do not feel anything. There is this thing called you get cremated when you passed and that is when they burn your body into ashes. Which is horrifying for me. But when I am alive and must decide if I wanted to be cremated or buried in the cemetery when I passed. What I want is whatever happens whatever happens. For me I just do not like making the decision on this type of thing. What I am trying to say somethings you must make the decision for even though you do not want to. Wish there is away where somebody can make the decision for me on this. These things I just do not like hearing when I am alive. What I like doing is to enjoy life. There is away someone can make the decision for me. But it is all up to me. When you get buried in the ground there is this thing called a graveyard. However, I believed you do not feel anything when you passed. All it is you feel scared, or you go peacefully in your sleep. Cannot really estimate on that because everyone is different. You cannot take any object to heaven other than you. Losing a loved one no one wants to go through that and especially pets and humans.

A lot can change within a second and that can be scary too. What you got to do is love much as you can. Sometimes you do feel lonely and scared without them. Being scared is a feeling of expression and other meanings of scared are terrified and horrified.

There is nothing we can change other than our feelings. We all feel scared and that is okay. Especially when it comes losing a loved one. However, there is another word called panic. Panicking is scary especially what happened to your loved ones and wondering why it happened to them. Is the scariest thing of all. We must protect our loved ones as much as we can. Always there for them when they need us. You always asked the question God and Jesus why you took my loved one away so soon. This is what I think and hopefully it will help you. For a fact I know no one wants to lose a loved one. But God and Jesus will protect them if your loved one is always kind and always do the right thing. They will be safe. There is a difference between an angel and a devil. A devil will harm things. But an angel will not harm anything. If your loved ones had done remarkable things. Guess what your loved one is an angel. Now a devil on another hand can be scary. Especially someone who harm your loved one. It will also be something so terrifying.

Knowing that devils are evil and if they harmed your loved one. Like any case preventing a murder. Of Course, there will be consequences, but it depends on the victim. By knowing who did it and that victim does not feel sorry or forgive that who harmed your loved one. Will go to hell for sure. Now if they do forgive, they might have a little chance if they correct in a way, they might have a chance to go to heaven. Heaven is a good place to go, and hell is a bad place to go. If the victim only cares about their selves and are very evil, then they will go to hell. Only if they do not care about anyone else. Is what I believed in writing this passage. We all have different opinions, and you might have a separate way of expressing it and that is okay. It is like yes; some unicorns can be evil and angels. Mostly of the dragons are evil. Yet again some can be angels. You just must take the good with the bad.

Another thing is that I do not like scary movies because they scare me and give me nightmares. Some things when it is Halloween some things scare me. Like for an example black cat. It is one thing that I will always be a scared of even when I was younger. For me I will never get over that fear. Every time I see a black cat, they make me jump and I get so scared. Even though not all cats scare me I have a beloved kitty named Ari and she is gray. The black cats scared me the most of all.

Chapter 6 Time

You never know how much lifetime you have with the loved one you about to lose. We never know how much time we have left on earth. Here is what we do we love and forgive. Yes, some things you will feel bad and regret. Sometimes you may forgive and never forget. You just must take the good with the bad. Always remember love is patient and love are kind.

Spending every hour and every second and minute. Until that human or pet takes their last breath. Then quickly your loved one has departed, and you feel aggrieved. It happened to me when I spend the last few minutes with my Papa. Also, it happens to all of us and that image you will never get out of your head. However, it will be stuck with you forever. What I am trying to say is that it may be frustrating and heartbroken. Even if that special loved one drive you crazy sometimes. Spend every second and minute with them and still love them no matter what. Even if they got on your nerves sometimes.

For a fact I know everything is going on all the same time. But the time you put in with the special loved one is what really matters. Time is limited but you got to have faith when the time comes as well. Time is one of the toughest things because that means life is going too fast and not waste any minute with the time of the loved one you about to lose. Time is what really matter the most. You must put in the time and be available for others. However, one day you may regret and wish oh I wish I spent more time with that special loved one. The reason is you never know how much time you have. What I wished for that is that time can be reverse, but the sad part is it cannot be reversed. Even if you cannot spend time with that loved one just call and just say hi how are you always thinking of you. Send letters and just send a message that is really all you must do. Time goes quickly and while other days go slow. Just remember to waste any time and let your loved one know you are always thinking of them. Time is the most important things in life. Time will come and go. But it is only your choice and decision how you want to control it. Spend much time as you can with your loved one. If you do not spend time with your loved one. Then how are you going to see each other in heaven. You may get a chance you may not. If you do not put in the time now is what I think. Time will not happen or less if you make it happen. However, time is one of the most valuable times in life. Time really does have it values. You got to make the time to make it more valuable. Make the effort to put in the time. Do not let time passed. Spend your heart and love with you special loved one. Time patient and kind are the most important things. It only up to you how you want to control it. No one else can except you.

Time is what you make it. Thinking of your loved one when they passed. You are putting in time thinking of them. You wish you had more time to spend with them. Like I said before if you did not spend enough time with your loved one. You might not see them again when you go to heaven. But if you did make time with your loved one that was alive. There is a chance you will see them again. This is what I think anyways it can be different. You will run into your loved one and the loved one will say I forgive you. But will never forget. Is what the loved one will say from heaven. There is no right or wrong answer this is my opinion and how I pictured it. You might have a different point of view and that is all right.

Chapter 7 Sadness, Rain and Emotions

When it rains it is your loved one from heaven crying. Also, God and Jesus as well. Is what I always think. Every raindrop you feel coming from the sky a loved one you lost is nearby. Just how we shed tears here on earth. Well, they shed tears in heaven in the sky. Now I know that no one knows where heaven is. But it is somewhere in the sky. It could be on the other side of the rainbow. Another place it could be a desert. Or on the other side of the mountain or the ocean or river. Heaven is just a mystery. It really can be anywhere. But will get more to that later. Anyways your loved ones may stop crying you have lost. It also may start again. You just must tell your loved ones you lost from their tears are crying from the sky. By telling them I am okay, and everything is great here on earth. You can stop crying now. Sometimes it will work if you believe and remain patient and positive. It takes a long time for the loved ones you lost that are in heaven to calm down.

Just like how we cry here on this planet called earth. The rain represents that your loved ones are thinking about you. Also, I am sure you are thinking of the same thing when you shed a tear here on planet earth. Yes, if it rains there will be pain and sadness. Sometimes you got to think rain in a positive way and not in a negative way. How our loved one's cry in heaven. Is how we cry on earth. We feel each other's pain. Just picture and think clearly in your mind that your loved ones who are gone are the rain and know that they are sad.

In both ways on earth or in heaven. No matter what you feel is sorrowful. Also, animals cry too even on earth or in heaven. Another word for it is called weeping. Then when your loved ones from heaven finish crying. Those tears also known as rain will turn into a puddle. Then boom in an instant and time of course your loved ones are healed and happy again. But what if we cry at the same time. Then we feel each other pain and sorrow.

What if the sun comes and dry all our tears away in heaven. We all have various levels of emotions. Some we can control. While other emotions we cannot. You will always have that pain when losing a loved one.

Even if there is no rain or sadness and no thunderstorm or lighting. There is still a chance your power can go out. It is your loved one coming to say hi. It happens to me a lot of times and it will happen to you too. For a fact I know rain, thunder and lightning can all be dangerous in a way. Then your mind just increases very quickly, and you start to worry. Dangerous weather I know it is not safe especially snow and hurricanes are not safe for anyone. But then you can realize the rain or snow, or hurricane can dry up. Either way there could be damage too. But will get more into that later. However, this is how I think of it your loved one from heaven will stop crying and the sun is another sign from your loved one. Coming to help you dry you up. Also, I do know the water from the rain or your loved one. May cause damage to any place. You may feel an insignificant damage inside of you. But your loved one will always be inside your heart.

Even if our loved ones make it hard for us. When they cry and water is everywhere. Just know that there is no limit. What I meant by that is us on earth is that our loved ones from heaven is sending us a message saying we all can help each other. Even through the tough times. Like bad storms just as a blizzard if you live in Pennsylvania which is where I from. Or if you are living in Florida or any state where there could be a hurricane. Just knowing keeping everyone safe and working as a team. What really matters the most. For a fact I know this. We are all not perfect. God and Jesus know that, and our loved ones know that. Even the water after the rain is also known as puddles is also a sign from our loved ones we lost. Yes, every situation is good and bad. But we all know we must take the good with the bad. The snow will melt but will never melt our loved one's hearts and ours. Including the rain and bad storms.

Rain can be a good thing while other times it can be a dreadful thing. Same as snow and hurricanes and there may be damage and I know it is not safe for anyone. But do not forget about your loved ones you have lost it could be a battle of a storm. Whatever, it is please do not you ever forget about them. They are always with you in your hearts. Also, they are watching over us as well. All you must do is to believe in that. Just must have the power and the strength. By expressing all those emotions together, it will have influence if you try. We may feel it at the same time or may not. Like I said we all have different balance levels. Just you got to find your purpose and that is what all matters the most. When I cry and another somebody cry, I can defiantly feel their pain. It is just a matter of time.

Is what I think in my own opinion anyway. We are all different. We are all not the same and that is fine as well. God and Jesus also know that. Including our loved ones as well.

Chapter 8 It is Hard

Yes, I believe it will always be hard losing a loved one. Will not be easy for sure. It is hard every day. If it is in the morning, afternoon, or evening. Not only that but when that special loved one is getting ready to pass away. Now that is the hardest part. It was for me especially seeing my Papa pass away. Again no one wants to go through losing a loved one. You never know what is going to happen. It is hard saying this. But sometimes or life is about choices and that loved is going through a tragic loss or preventing suicide. The sad part is there are ways we can help our loved one. But we cannot make the decision for them.

It is their choice if they want to damage their own body. For a fact I know that is hard. Not easy for sure. It is not your fault at all. The loved one just made an unwise decision. The loved one you about to lose or the loved one you already lost. We all been through it and the hardest part is that we cannot do anything about it. We cannot change each other's mind only you can. Now that is one of the hardest things. All you can do is to choose wisely. For a fact I know I have been through a loved one like that. Today I can still feel the sadness and the pain. We all wish we can have a second chance of life. But then all the sudden it is too late. We only live life once. Especially around the Holidays. Are the hardest times of all. Here on earth, they are no longer with you only in our hearts. They are in heaven celebrating it with God and Jesus. But the hardest part is that you cannot decide what your loved one to do. You can help them make the decision. However, they are the ones who must do it. If they make the right decision to help them, they might have a chance to live longer. My Papa made the wrong decision, and he did not get a chance to live longer by not doing chemo. Which is hard decision. Decision is never easy they are always hard. But the only person can decide is for yourself.

The hardest thing is that he is no longer living with me on earth. But I know he is in a suitable place called heaven with God and Jesus. He is in a safe place. Just as long Hell does not connect with heaven. That all what matters because Hell is an evil and bad place to go, and heaven is a great and happy place to go. The hardest thing is and which I hope not that there could be a chance, and this is just my point of view. You know how earth is not a safe place our world can be scary. Well, the different is in heaven. The angels can come cross to the devils. Yes, I believe in heaven the devils can still harm the loved ones or less if they have good security, it will be better. That is why we pray to have God and Jesus protect our loved ones that we lost. This is my opinion I can be completely wrong. But wherever you go it will always be hard and never will be easy. You just must pick the right route which is only your decision. But you can always ask for help. Like here on earth is always like heaven. However, the only difference is in heaven is by spiritually. But I do believe you will come a crossed to your loved one again when it is time for you to go.

Pets are always there when you need them. It is hard when that pet you loved so much. The pet that you lost is so hard. But again, will always be in your hearts. Suddenly, another one came along. However, that another pet will never replace the pet you lost before your new one. They just have different personalities just like us humans. At first it may be hard. But it only can get better.

Chapter 9 Will there be Pain God and Jesus Only knows

Can you feel pain when you or your loved one pass? At first you feel pain. The answer is yes and no. It depends on the human or pet. Once you go spiritually to heaven. That soul inside of you only God and Jesus will know. We all have different level of pain. Some feel pain while others do not. For a fact I know we all have different pain tolerance. It also means the loved one do not want you to suffer as well. When you go to heaven there will still be pain. One day I saw a bird and the bird went to heaven and I thought no longer in pain. Animals and humans once you go to heaven you will feel pain still. Now at first if you suffer with pain when you about to go to heaven at first you will feel pain. Then soon the pain will be gone for only a short amount a time and then it will start back up again. For me I thought the answer was no you will not feel no more pain. But then I realize the answer is true. Sadness means pain for sure. For an example what if that evil somebody put you in a tough situation and you still will feel pain not as much you will heal and forgive that someone, but you will never forget, and we all can learn something from this. Just like a hawk could of harm that little sweet bird.

Also, that human that who does not want to lose you feel pain as well. It is like when you leave the planet earth to go to heaven. God and Jesus will ask Why are you crying? You will say Why I am here? The reason is because the pain means not to be broken. When you go to heaven, God, and Jesus and all your loved ones you lost will be waiting for you. Even when you do go heaven is like your second life. The same thing you do on earth but spiritually. No matter what you are still going to have pain. What I believe peacefully is not an option. Or less if you go hear the waves in heaven now that is different that is peace. Yet again the pain will still come back of course you will still miss your loved ones who are living on earth. The question is will there be pain when you go to heaven the answer is yes. The no part of it that some will show it, and some will not. But we all have pain even when we do go to heaven. Jesus and God are the good side. The devils are the bad side. You will still feel that panic pain and be afraid and hope they do not come and attack you. This is my opinion and what I believed some may be true and some not. You will still feel pain no matter what place you go too.

Your loved ones on earth will feel pain because they miss you and you may feel pain because you miss them on earth. On earth you only get one chance of life or less if there is a magic cursed which there is not your second chance will be in heaven. You feel pain when you are on earth, and you will feel pain when you go to heaven. My opinion could be wrong, but you never know. Together we all can feel each other's pain no matter where we are. Including their sadness even if they do not show it. Just not humans but pets and all animals. Because if you are hurt then that other somebody is hurt as well.

Somedays you will feel sad and pain. While other days you feel happy with no pain and that is where you go to peace. They always say rest easy but that is never the case you will still feel pain spiritually. The pain will never ever go away. Even when you leave planet earth to go to heaven. My loved ones are still having pain because they are looking down at us from up above. You can still feel the pain and sadness in them.

Chapter 10 Follow the Signals

If you see stars in the sky or a shooting star. It is a sign that your loved one is near. Also, if you are sending a balloon up in the sky. You are thinking about your loved one. They will follow your heart. If you follow the stars. Or the signals. This will be amazing because our loved ones will follow back. Also, our loved ones we lost will always follow our hearts. We will always follow theirs as well. Now do not just follow the stars. Follow the birds as well. Cardinals and Blue Jays are a signal of your loved ones. Another signal to follow is if the leaves fall. It means that they are sending a signal or a message saying that they are with us.

There are so many signals to follow. Like if you find a dime on the floor that means our loved ones are safe and sending a signal. If you believe in the signals and know that your loved one is following you and is right beside you from heaven. It is amazing feeling to have knowing that they are with you wherever you go. When you think about them and believe just know that they are with you. Another signal is wind chimes. When you hear the wind chimes. Your loved ones are also nearby.

Another signal is when you see a butterfly that is a signal from your loved one from heaven thinking about you. The signals will come and go. But your loved ones will never leave your heart. Like when you light a candle, and you did not blow it out. Guess what it is a signal from your loved one. Also, when you hear voices and it sound like your loved one you lost. They are coming to say hi. It really amazing how all this works because if you believe in God and Jesus and still believe in the loved one you lost. They will never go away. They will always be with you no matter what. One day you will see them again face to face if you believe. You might have an image or signal in your mind that you can see them again.

Lastly, flags are a signal from your loved ones and all we must do is keep on waving those American flags for all the loved one we lost. That they will always be in our hearts, and they will never ever leave us. Just if you believe and not forget about them. Keep on thinking of the good times you had with your loved one you lost in heaven. Continue praying and wave those American flags and they will forever remain in your hearts. It is like your sending power to your loved ones in heaven and they are sending power back to you.

Chapter 11 To Guide

Our loved ones helped guide us. To find the strength to move forward with life. The loved ones will always be beside us wherever we go. Including God and Jesus as well. They will never leave our side. No matter what the situation might be. We always have God and Jesus in our lives and guess what it is the same thing with our loved ones we lost.

The stars will help guide us to wherever our loved ones are. Including a rainbow and a lit candle. Also, a reminder helps guide from a loved one as well. Something from the human or pet your loss. It could be their old clothes or something they like to do. For a fact I know not everyone like to be reminded of their loved one every second of the day. But sometimes it is a good thing. They are helping you guide you of the path you want to go. Unbelievably it helped me so much because a piece of my loved one that I lost always help me by guiding me where to go.

God and Jesus always guide you. Guess what so our loved ones does we have lost. You may not see them. But they are in your hearts helping to guide you. Like for an example the beach they are helping to guide you to get to the ocean to hear the waves. Then your loved one is right their beside you are guiding you on what path you want to chose in life. It really is up to you. They cannot make the decision for you. But they can help you by sending a message on a direction where you want to be. Or where you want to go. They will for sure help you.

However, guiding sometimes is not always a good thing. You see they are helping you and giving you pointers. But really it all comes down to you and the decision is yours. Also, guiding means diverse ways. Sometimes it may be your heart or that loved one you lost helped guide you. Also, your loved ones that you lost are the stars in the sky. Just talk to them like you do to God and Jesus and ask them I need help can you help guide me. Ask them am I making the right decision or am I making the wrong decision. My golden retriever Polly help guide me saying that everything in woof woof of course is saying everything is going to be okay. Woof woof I love you and will never leave your side. Then she blessed me with another Golden Retriever Flounder. Which I will get to that in another chapter.

There was also a lot of ways my Papa help guide me to. If it were not for him to help guide me and introduce me to Pickles, I would never ever like pickles. Do not knock it till you try it. He guides me in so many ways. Yes, some of them were bad that I do not say. Anyways, I have more loved ones I lost. Who had help guide me as well. Both of my grandpa and Papa always like to hear me sing and they are helping me and guiding me to not give up on my dreams. They taught me will including my parents too. Anyways, they tell me take every chance of life you can get. Sometimes things do not always work out. But it means never give up on it. If you fail the first time, try again. Life is all about that life is not a competition and know that no one is perfect. My tip to you to help guide you is that we all mess up and learn from our mistakes in life. The Lord and God and Jesus and your loved ones you lost will help guide you to move forward. The past can hurt but try not to forget about it. Yet again do not think about it every day. It is okay to think about it occasionally.

The darkness will help guide you in the light and that is including your loved ones you lost. There will always be a human and a pet to help guide you. Just remember what I am going to help guide you is everywhere temporary. Nothing will ever be permitted. So, if you must move just remember you're not alone and you will always have somebody. Yes, at first it can be hard, but you will have your loved one's help guide you. In another chapter I will get more into that. One-chapter close means a new one will help guide you. It can be anything guiding into a new adventure. You will always have your friends no matter where life guides you. Guiding to always make new friends as well. Also, guiding to not be stuck doing the same thing. But guiding to have more opportunities. Guiding to more possibilities is sometimes a good thing or it can be a dreadful thing. Helping to guide you is that you always must take the good with the bad. Yes, the guiding sometimes can take you in the wrong direction like getting frustrated at times that is okay we all are not perfect. Another way to help guide there are ways to help calm you as well. Guiding is never easy some points it will be hard and that is fine as well. One more thing you are only one human or pet and do not have magic powers and cannot be everywhere at once. Guiding to make plans is the most important thing to keep in mind. It may not be something you like but guiding to take nothing for granted. Help guide you if you must cancel some things in life, it is an ok sometimes. But do not do it all the time. To help guide there is always a reason. Sometimes again to help guide you got to respect that decision at first you may get mad, but you will get over it and help guide you to move forward. To help guide do not waste or lose anytime.

Chapter 12 The Way I Picture Heaven

The way I picture heaven is that our loved ones we lost on earth. They are doing the same thing what we are doing. However, the difference is they are doing it spiritually. Heaven is a beautiful place if you close your eyes. You can really imagine heaven. Now heaven is a mystery. No one really knows where heaven is. What I heard in my life is wherever the location you passed that is where you go to heaven. Like it can be on a mountain or in the field wherever the location may be and wherever you end your life that is where you will go to heaven and there is this thing called an afterlife. Which I will explain in just a few moments. But however, I have this feeling that you got to start somewhere.

There are two worlds when you passed one is called heaven. While the other one is called hell. The difference is heaven is where the angels are. Hell is where are. Now, I believed if you do good and believe that there is a God and Jesus. Then you will go to heaven and become an angel. If you are bad and do dreadful things and do not believe that there is a God and Jesus. Then you are a devil, and you will go to hell. But I also know this some humans do not go to church in their life. But they still believed in God and Jesus. It could be that they do not have transportation to get to church. You will have God and Jesus wherever you go and same with your loved ones. Heaven may be far away. But in your heart, it is not far away. You just got to follow your loved on and their footsteps. All you must do is believed and your loved ones are right there with you that you lost. By seeing valleys and mountains there they are with you no matter where life takes you.

Back to the afterlife. What I believed an afterlife to me is that when you get to heaven. You will be doing the same thing as you are here on earth. But only spiritually. Yes, I believed heaven it will be different from earth. Now hell that is completely another story. If you do charitable deeds, you will be going to heaven. In life you just must remember to take the good with the bad. Even when you see snow or see the ocean you can take the time and think what heaven means to you. We all express it in a unique way. If you do dreadful things in life and still believed in God and Jesus, there will be a chance that you will still be able to go to heaven. Only if you believed that there is a God and Jesus and by asking for their forgiveness of what you had done. We all have a good and bad side of us. It is up to you how you control it. We all learn, and we all make mistakes. Some things you can fix and some things you cannot. But it never to late to fix those things. Each and every one

Chapter13 Love

When you lose your loved ones. They won't be gone forever. You will always love your loved ones no matter what. Even if the situation is hard. It could be family or friends. Your heart may feel a little broken because they are no longer with you on earth.

When you fall on to the ground. Sometimes your loved ones from heaven catch you and sometimes they don't when you fall. The love and laughter will always be in our hearts. Once your loved one you lost or going to lose. They will always love you and you will always love them. The love will never go away. Just locked all the memories and good times. You have in your heart and mind. Don't ever forget them. Even they are no longer with you they will always love you. If you have a lot of love, you are an angel for sure. The balloons you send up in the air. You are sending to your loved ones in heaven. Always remember them and just remember the love and bond you have with them. Light up those phones sending your loved ones in heaven and to let them know that you loved and miss them. Including lighting a candle as well. Will show the love and power and to know that you are thinking about them and love and miss them. Your loved ones in heaven still miss you too. The love and relationship you had with them and share with them. Will never ever be forgotten.

You are fighting for your loved ones and your loved ones from heaven are fighting for you. Keep on making those snow angels if you live in a place where there is snow. Or if not make a sand angel. It is sending love to your loved ones you lost. There is a lot of power of love to send to your loved ones in heaven. Always love your loved ones from the moon to back. Don't forget to smile to your loved ones and put on a happy face. Your loved one always don't want to feel your sadness. It is ok to be sad sometimes. I still feel sad from losing my loved ones. As well and your loved ones you lose. Don't have to be by blood. It can be anyone. If you lost a pet always love that pet, you lose as well. Just love from your heart. Even though sometimes it can feel broken inside. Love and cherish those memories with the loved ones you lost.

You may experience fear of losing a loved one and it is scary all at the same time. But also, you need to have the strength of losing a loved one. For a fact I know it won't be easy. Back in chapter 9 I talked about that in heaven your loved one will still have pain. The reason is because they are feeling your sadness. They are feeling your pain. Now you won't have any more pain from your injury. But the pain in the sadness of your heart. Yet again they want the pain in your heart to heal and to have a happy heart. Your loved ones will love you. If you do good things and believe in God and Jesus. God and Jesus will love you too. Love is wild and show it with proud to your loved ones you lost. Your love is the light and the brightness and the spark. Just don't lose the love inside your heart. Love is pure and with the kindness and strength you will be ok in life. Your loved ones will from heaven above will always be by your side and help guide you. Just must follow your loved one's footprints. Let the love from the rain fall on you because it is your loved ones from heaven. Sending their love to you. The love will never be the same, but it will always be in your heart. Keep on letting the glory of your love shine. Your loved ones you lost from heaven will be proud of you no matter what. You can take love wherever you go and there are different ways to show it for sure. Love is a dream and an obstacle. Showing and caring and loving are the most valuable things in life. Yes, love may have it ups and downs. By showing the kindness of heart is what matter the most. We all can feel each other pain in love from heaven or the loved ones that are still with us on earth. Around the Holidays showing the love for a child patient with cancer by giving them a gift. Or donating food to the homeless. You are putting power of love into your heart to those loved ones and their families. Some of them may not have families. You are like family to them. Like I said family doesn't have to be by blood. Yes, for sure it can break your heart. But at the same time, it is making you feel so good. You just must build that confidence of love. By doing that is just showing it.

Love is a gift from the heart. The power of your goodness what matter the most. Mean heart are not good. Devils are not good they don't have good heart like angels do. If you do goodness in your heart, you will be okay.

Chapter 14 Hope

Back in the last chapter I forgot to mention my pet that I lost Polly love. But there is always hope because another one comes along. Well guess what their will always be hope for your loved ones no matter what. In the morning, afternoon and in the evening. Also, it is good to hope for that loved one to get better. Even if they about to go to heaven. Just hope that our loved ones are doing good even if they are no longer with us here on earth. For an example I hoped my Papa could have lived longer and my other loved ones. But it didn't happen. You just must take the good with the bad. Just hope they are doing well in heaven.

Also, it is good to hope for that loved one to get better. Even if they about to go to heaven. Just hope our loved ones are doing good. Even though if they are no longer with us here on earth. Hope that Jesus and God are spreading the love and goodness to them in heaven.

Spread the love and hope for all who passed away from cancer. No one wants to go through cancer. Even spread love and hope for children who have cancer. All you can do is to have hope for them and all you can do is pray for them. Some may pass away from cancer, and some may survive. Just have hope for all and spread the love to their families. Those who don't make it just have hope and love that their loved ones are watching over them including God and Jesus. Including pets as well that who had cancer. Their some power you can put in. Which all you can do is pray and have hope and spread the love. My wish for them is that I hope and can spread the love by going and putting on a show for them and giving them gifts. My Papa went through lung cancer and didn't make it. All you must do is love and hope for them. It melts my heart seeing these humans and pets or all animals going through cancer.

But all I can do is the same thing you are doing have hope and spread the love for them. If you put hope and love into your heart and praying for them. Doing all you can. You are doing the right thing. By donating you are doing the right thing. Anything by helping you are doing the right thing. Now I am saying you don't have to do it all the time. Every time you do it. It is a blessing of hope and spreading love and that is what called a pure heart. So, give yourself a hand because you are doing the right thing. Praying is another sign of hope and spreading the love too. Just have hope and spread the love out of your heart and hope for them to get better if not and they end up going to heaven and leaving earth. All you can do is to say God and Jesus please keep my loved one safe in God and Jesus we say amen. Hope that God and Jesus have good hands with them. Just say this isn't a goodbye just see you later. The 3 power so far are Pray, Hope, and spread the love. Also, have a good and great power of the goodness of your heart. Just know that hope and love won't let your loved ones down. All you can do is put in the effort and try. An also, bring hope to families that can't afford a Christmas and help donate a toy so everyone can have a great Christmas. Now that will be a gift from the heart to help what they need.

Chapter 15 Faith

You always got to have faith to find strength to carry on after losing a loved one. Strength will give you courage to carry on and move forward with your life. Before we get to the other chapters. What I want to do is take the time and go back to Chapter 2 Faith over Fear. All I can say is this you have to have the faith to come over that fear and to conquer it. Now back to the other ones. You have to have love, hope and faith for your loved ones. All of those words are showing power. We will talk about each topic clearly.

By starting out with love. If you show the power of love guess what you have a good / great heart. It is called unfailing love. Your love will never fail. Congratulations by showing love you are doing the right thing. Now I am not talking about boyfriends or girlfriends. What I am talking about is you and how you are expressing your love and how you are showing it. If it is helping someone out that is one thing you are doing to spread love. This book is not about dating it is about to help you to find the love inside of you. Love is patient and love is kind. By showing and helping you are on the right track and on the right page. Maybe someone drop their books and a bully is starting to call names and you stop and help that somebody. Stand up for them and lend a helping hand. Now that is showing love and you have a pure heart, and it makes you feel good and that other someone feel good. That bully will realize hopefully that bully will apologize and said what did I do wrong and how can I fix this. You get another chance to do better. Even the pain will still be there. If you see someone get hurt same things like falling on the ground. Taking the time and helping. You get a redo by doing better to have a great heart and show love. By working as a team.

Now on to hope to find the strength and hope for the best. Hope your loved ones are doing great. Find the hope and courage inside of them. Also, hope they can accomplish their goal. Praying and hoping for that somebody to get better. That is showing the goodness and greatness of your heart. Hope they can get through what ever they are going through.

Lets talk about faith now. Then will put them all together. Faith if you have faith that you can do all things through Christ who strengthens me you have a good and great heart and doing all you can. Faith takes courage and strength and time. You can have some help for sure. But it all depends on you and how you can control it.

It is time to go back through and put all the 3 out of 4 is how I put it words and topics and together and they all mean something as well. The 3 powers are Love, Hope and Faith and if all of those don't work just pray. If you do all of those things. You have a good/ great heart. If you don't all you have to do is change to put the effort and time. That why I am saying 3 out of four because. Love and hope and faith you have to try and if it doesn't work have a plan b and pray to put in the effort and time and then you can feel power in your heart. Also, showing love, hope and faith by showing the light in your heart in the darkness. One of the greatest powers of all is every power I named. It changes what we do and who we are and that is just a great feeling. We are all not perfect. We celebrate life in our own unique way. That is the greatness and power of our heart. Praying for a second chance to do better is a blessing. Amen to all of that. Just saying to God and Jesus you are never going let me down. But there is a way you can let yourself down. But if you believe and fix those things you will never let yourself down and that is another way showing power within yourself. If you do all of those things, you are on the top of the world and top of the cross. Now I do have a disability but that doesn't define me who I am because we are all unique in our own way and pureness of our heart by showing love hope and faith will never let us down. Just want to get a shout out to all who have a disability you matter, and you are who you are and what you a meant to be in your own unique way. (: Hope, Faith and love are my favorite words and topics to talk about. Praying is also my favorite thing to do because it helps me believe in the power of Hope, Faith, and love. By having a great pure heart is what makes me happy. That is all what I can say.

Chapter 16 Wish to visit Heaven

Sometimes here on earth we wish to visit our loved ones in heaven. If only that wish came true would be great. Or we wish that our loved ones can just spend one day with us from heaven. Also, wish to spend time with them again by blowing out a candle every year for your birthday and saying I just want to spend time with the loved one I lost by visiting heaven. Or my loved one comes to earth. If only if there is away the sadness is that there is not away. Every possible answer you can think of there is no way.

Even for the Holidays there is no way. All you can do is visit them in your dreams. But sometimes I always believed my loved ones I lost are there. It is like I can really see them. Even if someone grant you 3 wishes it won't work. Which is hard and sad. Yes, it can be heartbreaking. But you can always go and talk to them. The way you talk to God and Jesus. You can make multiple wishes, but they won't come true. Or less if that wish turns into a Miracle.

A miracle means to me something out of the blew that is a surprise. It could be a Christmas miracle. Or any kind of miracle you can think of. A miracle from heaven now that is a blessing and that would be cool to see our loved ones again. But we only can see them in our minds and our hearts. Or by picturing them up in the sky. That is why you must keep busy, and it is always good to remember your loved ones. Even if you have 16 wishes there is no way.

The stars in the sky at nighttime is your loved ones. Around Christmas time I like to remember the good times that I had with my loved ones from the past. By looking at the Christmas tree. Sometimes it helps me if I write it down. One way is that you can write down the memory you had with your loved one and put it on the tree. Unbelievable I just gave myself a great idea and hope it will help you too.

If not, there are other ways like if your loved one passed and the last gift you got from them that you don't want to get rid of keep it. It is a good reminder from your loved one. However, if you don't like reminders then get rid of it. But think wisely because one day you will regret it. Of course, not I can't grant wishes for you loved ones to come back. But I can give you some tips and ways to help you. Another way is writing in your diary if you have one. Or looking back at pictures and videos. Another way is singing a song. Or talking to someone about losing a loved one and by talking about having memories with that loved one will help so much. It may not but you never know less you try. By going to hear the waves and looking back on the memories will help or listening to the wind. You may lose sight of your loved one for a quick sec. But it will come back to you. Because you might be busy of thinking about something else. Right now, you live on earth and that is your home and your loved one's home is in heaven. You got to realize homes are temporary. Wherever you are you won't be there forever.

There is also this thing called a miracle worker. The meaning of a miracle worker means someone can create miracles to happen. It can be anyone just not your loved one. Miracles comes out of nowhere. It means there is a miracle that can fix it. You just must put work into it to make it happen. The only thing is you can't bring your loved one back from heaven. But there are other ways. Like a miracle is remember something special and memory you did with your loved one. Or you can go see a medium. Well, I have a secret that is very deep I can hear my loved one voices, and I know my loved ones are there. Every time I try to meditate that is all I see in my mind. What I do is I do see them spiritually. That is why I don't really sleep that good at night. Believe it not it comes from your heart in your mind. What I do try is think about something else when I meditate but it doesn't always work that way from me. The way it works for me to clear my mind is walking and running or watching movies which is not healthy sometimes. Now here is the hard part I am about to say, and I am going to let it out. Sometimes and now, I am not saying all the time. The thing is I do talk to dead, and I can't ever get there spirit out of my mind. But we are here voices it can be our loved ones or just an imagination which are two different things. Me I don't have an imaginary friend. So, the voices I hear in my head are my loved ones and other people loved ones. That is why I don't like to go to cemeteries because all I can do is feel my loved ones I lost and other loved ones they lost pain.

That is why I keep it a secret inside of me and I don't like scaring people it is my silence that make it happen. That is why I am learning how to talk in American sign language base on practice. But my dream is to be an actor and that is why I am working on saving my voice and I also do Ted talks and theatre the reason why I don't talk that much because I want to save my voice and I do hear spirit voices in my head. My silence is that I am not trying to scare you. Sometimes I get scared too we all do. The only way is to apologizes and that is it and move on. Meditating is supposed to calm me, but it doesn't work for me. But it does mean it might can work for you. However, it doesn't for me.

Chapter 17 Why we can't go with our loved ones

One reason is that we can't go with our loved ones to heaven. Where our loved ones had gone too. Is because our loved ones want us to stay on earth and continue to live our lives. You can go to heaven one day. Just not right now. Here on earth, you got plans even if they don't work out. Also, you got goals to accomplish. Yes, it may be time for your loved ones to go. But it is not the time for you to go with them right now.

When my first golden retriever was about to passed, she didn't want to leave earth to go to heaven and I keep on telling her I can't go to heaven with you right now. That golden retriever was my Polly love. It was one of the hardest things to say to her. That is why she inspired me to write this book. Now if you pass away all together then you go to heaven together. Which no one wants that to happen. You never know what life will do to you. But what I can say is make sure you protect yourself. It is a scary world out there. All you must do is fine your safe zone.

Take every chance and opportunity in life and always try something new. They call me the everything girl because I do a little bit of everything. Now I was never on a tennis team. But I do know how to hit a tennis ball. Let me tell you I came from a small town called Warren Pa. What I did I learn everything what they have taught me, and I still remember the things I did. It is where I grew up and I try new things what I like but the plan never worked out I can't stick with that one sport. If you start something finish it and don't quit. Try it a few times and if it doesn't work out. Guess what it doesn't work out and that is where you move on to something else. For me I like performing but I also like to do sports to keep me active and by the time I get home I am tired. What I always say is don't knock till you try it.

We can't go to heaven with our loved ones right now because our loved ones want us to stay on earth and continue to live our lives. If you are tired of doing the same thing do something else. That is another way how you can clear your mind. Do something good. Don't do something bad. Now I can't control you what you can do only you can. But I can help you base on my experiences. But the humans on earth with you right now can encourage you. Your loved ones to from heaven above from inside of your heart. Everywhere I live, I like to learn something new. Learning something new is a great thing. Even if you must relearn it. It is not a bad thing. It always good to have challenges where you try to figure out before you ask for help. That is why my life is based on practice. If you don't practice and study, then how do you expect to get better. Trying to still get my driver's license and I am not giving up on it. Don't quit and don't you ever give up. There are a lot of possibilities out there for you and you just got to find your calling. Even if it takes time to make it right and do it right. Your grace whatever you do is enough. Bring on the joy for others. Maybe they are going through a bad time. Maybe they say they don't want to talk about it and that is when you must respect that and maybe they don't want to talk at all. It is all called respect and respect what you have with others. But always listen what they got to say, and they say hurtful things to you just walk away. Working on writing music and songs that may help you. They will be out there to the world. Just working on getting my recording studio. That is why I am keep my own songs to myself. If you want your dreams to happen, you got to work for it and save for it. We all have different goals and dreams the only way to pursue them is up to you and by putting in the hard work. We can't go to heaven with our loved ones right now. But we will one day meet again. Right now, they remain in our hearts.

Nothing can change that. But I am telling you right now it is not your time to go. God and Jesus will love you forever just as long you don't do something evil. Also, your loved ones you lost that went to heaven or still with you here on earth. Will help you carryon and help you move the direction where you want to go in life.

Chapter 18 Don't have Magic Powers

The truth is that none of us have magic powers. But as we do wish though. However, there are angels, and the power of our loved ones is what gives us power. God and Jesus will give our loved ones we lost power and love and hope and faith to carry on.

My Papa was a huge fan of Superman. But my Papa didn't have magic power. His magic power is love and hope and faith he had. He left earth and want me to be his super girl. All our power is love and hope and faith. He always like helping others and I like doing the same thing. Helping others just make you feel great inside and having power inside of your heart. What matters the most of all. Sometimes if you did it before you can do it again for sure I believe you can. By showing power of love for others and having hope for others and faith means strength to carry on. Those are my magic powers, and they may be the same for you too. Sometimes you just must go back to the beginning where you first believed in something.

To have faith it gives you the power to have strength and to have courage and once you believe that. Then you can believe again and again. The greatness of the power of love is the most powerful thing of all. Also, having hope is another powerful thing of all as well. Even if it doesn't work at least you are trying. Faith will guide you to strength from your heart and that is what a superhero is all about.

You can be your own superhero. You have the power to control you and only you. No one else can do it for you. If you are helping others, you are on the right track and doing the right thing.

Your magic power comes from your heart. We all believe and see things at a different point of view. But what if we put our magic powers together and work as a team. Now you might be doing the right thing. But it is up to that other somebody to do their part. We can't control anyone other than ourselves. We are all different in our own unique ways.

The way we can connect our powers is by working together with one another. By putting our minds and hearts together that is the most magical power ever. Even if that somebody gets on your nerves only you can bounce back, and it is up to that human to bounce back and to find their power again. Now we are all one person and the magic part of it we can't do is be at every place at once. We can't do everything all at once. To tell you the truth it takes time. For me it is okay to have reminders but again sometimes I just don't like humans remind me. It will happen when I get to it. It takes time for me to process things and sometimes others don't get that in me. If we rush things, then how are we going to do a great job. That is why you need to slow down, and we all move at a different paste and take your time. Now if I forget something then you can remind me. But just give me time. What I am saying is that I am not trying to show attitude. But that happens when you try to rush me. You see for an example if someone is a slower learner have patient with them. Give them time please. Or if that human is in a hurry, then you have a challenge to move quickly and move the power in you. The more power and time we have with somebody will be the best power ever in the world by helping one another.

Chapter 19 Change and Better

Change is hard. It takes us awhile to experience change. That special loved one that is not here with us on earth anymore. When the human or pet no longer on earth with you. Change will never heal. But we got to learn to overcome it. Change is never easy, and it will never be easy. But change can be a good thing sometime. Your loved one you lost will never be forgotten. Now I am not talking about the money part of making change. Maybe sometimes we don't like change. So, we stick with the same thing.

But for me I like change because it is better even if it takes some time, and it will. It just doesn't happen overnight. Change can be a great thing and change can also be a bad thing. The only way is to give change a chance and by experience it if it doesn't work out with new change and you are not happy. Then you can go back to your old ways.

But just give it time and the better you will be. It can be the time change. The bad part is that your loved one that you lost are no longer with you on earth. They are now in heaven. You don't see them every day like you normally do. But they will never leave you. They will always be with you no matter what. If there is a job, you're not happy with you got to look at the bad and good side of it and no that every job is temporary it may never be a forever job for you. But you must be thankful of that change and give it time and a chance. Just be thankful of that change taking a big step and just be thankful that you have a job. If it is not a job for you keep searching because something better will come up for you, I promise you.

My dog Polly passes away the year 2022 but I was blessing with another golden retriever Flounder, and it is a huge change for sure. But that other pet you have will never be replace. Change can be tricky but just give it time before you move on.

Just by having hope for that change to get better. Like it can be a drink someone made that you don't like. But the change is that human saying oh I hope they like my drink I made and hope they like it. If not, then I can make that new change and do better next time. Maybe I mess up on an ingredient and that's okay. You just got to change for the better and that is what you got to do. Make change to not make that same mistake again. Hopefully this make sense to you if not give me feedback on this book and I would like to fix and make that change better for you.

Chapter 20 Gift

A gift is like from the heart. Now I am not talking about the gifts you get on your birthday or for Hanukah and for Christmas. For an example blessing are and I am about to tell you why. My first golden retriever as I repeat went to heaven. Then I was blessed because a new golden retriever came along. Now I am saying that my first golden retriever will never be replaced with my second. They totally have different personalities.

A gift is like the waves from the ocean and hearing the waves it is a gift. That our loved ones are nearby. Or a gift is something you can give to someone without payment. Like helping them out with something. Or making something homemade from your heart and by being thankful that you are healthy and strong. It can be a gift from your loved one from heaven. By a sign from your loved one from up above. If you get a gift from someone, be grateful and thankful. What that human gives you. You are gift from God and that what you are. Just not me that I am a gift from God but everyone.

For me I like giving then receiving. If someone need something I am right, there. A gift does come from the heart, and it makes you feel good. The gift comes from your heart and up above. A gift is making sure you have water. What I like to do is make sure everyone is taking care of. But sometimes I am so busy taking care of others and sometimes I forget to take care of myself. Make sure you give a gift to yourself too and make sure you make time for yourself. That is why you need to take breaks to renew yourself and that is a great gift. So, this Holiday season take the time and be thankful of the gifts you got. Don't be like I didn't want a book. I wanted a play station. Be thankful of what you get. Try to help your parents even if you don't want to because they are giving everything to you what you need, and they are trying. If it something you don't like don't get mad at them. If you can't afford a gift, make something for them or help them out whatever they need help with. For a fact I know parents gets on your nerves even my parents get on my nerves but the best gift you can give is love. Even if I argue I still love my parents no matter what.

Take that gift from the heart and have a thankful heart. We all can learn something about this. Or a gift is something you can sing or do based on talent. Now that is a gift as well.

Chapter 21 Ways to Over Come

There are ways you must overcome losing a loved one. The first one is having faith which is strength and knowing that they are going to be okay, and you are going to be okay. Sometimes you must overcome thinking about this and knowing ways how to over come it. One way for me is that I always switch things and do something else to get my mind off my loved one that I lost. By knowing that I will see them again.

But for now, it is time to focus on the humans who are in front of me here on earth and I am talking about pets as well. The ones I see in sight and my surroundings. What I do is try to not think of my loved ones from heaven. However, what I do is learn how to over come it and express my feelings to others. Yes, we are all in the same boat. We all must learn to overcome these battles. Of course, there will be times you do think of your loved ones. But try to not think of them all the time.

It will never be easy for you or for me. Once you lose that loved one in the battle. It will always be stuck with you, and it won't go away. But you must learn to overcome it and that is having strength inside of you. You must overcome and know that God and Jesus are in good hands with your loved ones. Just trust them and know they are taking really good care of your loved ones. Maybe taking your mind off it and do something big from your heart and keeping yourself busy with other things. Instead of talking to your loved ones take a break and talk to God and Jesus instead. That is why we have different hobbies in our life to keep us busy.

Keep life moving and going. Or doing something that makes you think. You will see your loved ones when you see them. Lift things up and learn how to overcome them. Now there are probably more ways I don't mention. Like bake a cake that will help you overcome. Or going to the mall hanging out with your friends. Just focus on your freedom that you have or writing things about you down in your journal. Overcome the darkness and into the light by living and enjoying life. Just don't be afraid to overcome the obstacles you may have. You will never be the same. But the way is that you must overcome it. Just overcome and know your loved ones will always be with you and live by faith. Just know nothing is impossible. But it is your loved ones and God and Jesus who gives you strength and others too. Just got to put your minds together. Overcome the lack of energy and change it because it is never too late to start over.

Over coming on things will help you so much in life. If you just see for yourself to overcome them. It takes time for sure to overcome things for sure. It won't happen within a day. Maybe it takes one thing at a time. Not to do everything at once.

Over coming on things takes patients and pride. Overcoming is not easy. It is hard but it will get better by overcoming the new with the old. These are some of the ways. Of course, there are more as well.

But these are the only ones I can think of.

Chapter 22 Shine

As you continue to shine here on earth. Your loved ones continue to shine in heaven. Just like the sun. They shine so brightly in the sky. They are like lights in the darkness. Shining bright like stars at night. Or you shine bright like the colors of the rainbow in the sky. By shining bright like a diamond. Shine bright like a rocket or fireworks. Whatever kind of light could be.

It can be a light bulb you shine like. Or a lantern or a flashlight you shine at night. It also can be a lit candle. It may be lights on a Christmas tree. But whatever it is your light will always shine. It will never burn out. Be the hope of the light and shine.

Shining will make you more powerful if it is here on earth or in heaven. No matter where God and Jesus will see you shine. Including your loved ones. You shine bigger and brighter wherever you go.

Nothing will change you how you shine to the world. Shine is a sign of happiness and glory ness. Shining the light from your mind and heart and the smile will help you shine as well. By standing up tall will make you shine. Just think of the song. This little light of mine I am going to let it shine every day. Or the song I am walking on sunshine. Those songs can help you have a positive impact on your life and make you shine. Taking care of yourself that will make you shine and have power. Shine and don't let anyone get in your way.

Find your own path and light to shine on earth or in heaven. Either way your light will not burn out. Your light will never turn off I promise you it will keep shining. Just be you and keep shining your light to your loved ones you lost and to the whole world.

Keep and always carry that smile and that potential in your life. Especially when you do get to heaven as well. Shine like no other. If you don't shine bright now there is time to change that. Help someone else be the light. The light will make you feel good and shine in others. This is a promise you can't break for sure. Keep shining in the sky.

Chapter 23 Spirit/ Ghost/ Angels

As you may already know this. But there are ways you can see your loved ones if you believe. Now you may not believe right away. But you can feel their spirit in with you. When you pass your loved ones turn into ghost. Their bodies are spiritually. Or they can change into angels as well. For an example I know my old golden retriever her spirit is living in my new golden retriever. It is just amaze me so much. Some don't believe me.

But I can really feel it. When the power goes out at places it is a ghost. Or it can be what is called the holy ghost which mostly happens in churches. But it also means when the power goes out our loved ones are watching us. Our spirits of our loved ones are coming for us. Ghost can be scary. But your loved one's won't harm you they are angels. Just like Casper the friendly ghost. Now if they do harm you that is a different story.

Like if they come from heaven, they won't harm you. But if they come from Hell, they are evil and devils and they will harm you. So, you got to be careful with that. If they come from heaven, they are angels. Every time when the power goes out, I always say it is okay it is just our loved ones coming to say hi. They are coming to check on us. Even when we are sleeping because they know when you are awake. They know if we been bad. They are always watching us even though they are gone. They may pop up in your car or wherever. Your loved ones will never lose sight where you are. They may pop up anytime they want. When you pass and wherever you pass that means that your spirit leads you to. Well, the start anyways and then you move around. They also known as orbs too.

There spirit will live on forever even into the next future. They move like we move only in a different way of course. Each of them is their own. But also, God and Jesus Spirits as well. Their favorite holiday from heaven which are angels is Christmas. They are up there partying with our Savior Jesus Christ and celebrating his birthday. You know what Jesus he died on the crossed for us. Now the devil favorite Holiday come and haunt you is Halloween. Which they are from Hell. This is what I believe and hope it helps you. The angel from heaven comes in your dreams. While the devils come from Hell and that is a living nightmare. Spirits, ghost, Angels, and Devils are different things. Well ghost and spirits are like the same thing to me. But Angels and Devils are different to me. Angels won't harm you but devils will for sure.

When you pass it is the same thing. If you do good, then you become an angel. Also, you will go to heaven as well. If you are bad to the bones, then you will go to Hell and be a devil which mean by harming others in away. Look we all have a good / bad side. Just as long you don't harm others you will be fine. This is all I have to say about this chapter our loved one's spirits will always be with us and not go away.

Chapter 24 Last Day on Earth

Your loved one's last day on earth is very depressing. You know you're about to lose them and is their last day. What you got to do is make every moment count and cancel plans if you have too. Just to be with them one more time when they are alive. Until they take that last breath, and their ticket gets pulled. You must be with them every step of the way.

Then when they gone that is where the tears come. You may cry for days or months. But you got to find the strength to carry on. No one wants their special loved one to leave earth. But you know we all don't live forever we wish we did. But we don't. Even your pets don't live forever.

The last day on earth you just got to make it special for that loved one. It can be a family member or a close neighbor or friend. You got to make every second count. That loved one that supposed to be living and became ill. You never know because you got to love as much as you can.

Chapter 25 Always in Our Hearts

Our loved ones will always be in our hearts no matter what. Wherever we go in life. Which is work, doctors' appointment or vacation. They will be in our hearts wherever we go. Even to the beach or in the woods. Our loved ones will never leave us. They will always remain in our hearts. They will always be locked away in our hearts. Just a heads up and know that the last chapters are going to be short. That is all I have for this one and that they will always guide us in our hearts. If they are alive or not, they will always be with us.

You will have a good heart if you believe in that heart and know that our loved ones are inside our hearts. Even when we leave to go to heaven they will always remain in our hearts. It will always be everlasting.

Chapter 26 Lucky

Life is full of surprises because when you lose a loved one. You get lucky because another comes along. We lost our beloved golden retriever female named Polly. But we got lucky because now we have a male golden retriever name Flounder.

One time I was playing a game with my friends, and I always got lucky when I role the dice from my loved ones from heaven and that is a miracle for sure. They help me by playing the game and I know it was my loved ones from heaven who made me feel lucky. I got so lucky that I end up winning. Sometimes it feels good when you feel lucky. Just like a lucky duck is how I put it. Sometimes in life you do get lucky. Just like a lucky charm as well. Sweet like candy is another way of lucky. This chapter is short and sweet. At some point in our lives, we feel lucky. Just not me but everyone.

Chapter 27 Fly High

Now back to my Papa he loved Superman and I always think I am Supergirl. Here is why when my Papa left earth to go to heaven. He flies high in the sky and left all his loved ones behind. Now I know this is fantasy which I know none of us have superpowers. What I forgot to mention in the other chapters when you become a spirit you can fly. When you go to heaven. Here on earth, you got to walk on your feet or move around in a different way. But this is my story I am sharing with you. My Papa put on that red cape and flew in the sky all the way to heaven. What I always say is Fly high which means your flying like a bug or a bird in the sky. Like spreading those wings like an angel. Or of course flying like an airplane.

Chapter 28 Control

None of us have control of losing a loved one. If their time to go then it is their time to go. Only you can control you no one else can. Your control is based on your decision. It is your choice if you want to work hard by putting in the effort. Yes, you can control your animals, but it is up to your animals as well. We can't control our loved ones to live longer. Every step of the way we can't control anything except for ourselves We all lose control sometimes on things. But another word for this is called self-control. We all respond to it differently. Especially when it comes to losing a loved one. Sometimes you move forward with it and sometimes it comes back to you. That is not a bad thing. For an example still till this day I couldn't get over of losing my Papa. Just know losing a loved one is not your fault. You have no control on that. This is all I have to say about control. For a fact I know it is hard losing a loved one and know that it is not your fault, and you may think it is may not.

But we all struggle with any type of control. God and Jesus know we are not perfect and that we all are not the same and to know we are unique in our own kind of way. But we can't control anyone except for ourselves. That is all I have on control hope you learn something out of it. Sorry, to say this I can't control you all I can do is control myself and we all express it differently. But I can help you by giving you some tips and I happen to know one right now. Take 3 big breaths to calm yourself down and it may take longer than others. Yes, control is hard, and it is never easy. Now it is time to take 3 big breaths to the next and final chapter of this book.

Chapter 29 Memories/ Conclusion

At Christmas time it will never be the same with our loved ones we lost. But I will always have the memories with them. Now it is time for them to celebrate it in heaven with God and our savior Jesus. The year 2022 will be the first Christmas without my golden retriever Polly. But it will be my second golden retriever Flounder first Christmas. Polly, I enjoyed spending Easter with her in 2022. Was one of the last major Holidays. Yes, from the previous years I enjoyed celebrating every Holiday with her. But now I can spend the Holidays with my new golden retriever Flounder. The love and memories will not go away will always remain in our hearts.

Especially all the loved ones I have lost will hold a special place in my heart. This year 2022 will be hard and sad. But also, happy because our loved ones have a great life. Hopefully this book you will learn something, and we all can learn something from it as well. I learn a lot of things by writing this book and I hope it helps you. All the memories from the past you won't lose them. You will always have those treasures locked away in your heart.

Even a Parachute and windmill or blowing bubbles you are sending the love and magic to your loved ones in heaven. What I promise you your loved ones will always be around and forever remain in your hearts.

Bible verses

Can do all things through Christ who gives me strength

Philippians 4:11-13

The Lord is close to the brokenhearted and saves those who are crushed in Spirit.

Psalm 34:18

He will wipe every tear from their eyes

Revelation 21:4

of us is not perfect and do not ever forget that.

There is one more thing that I learned that makes me sad and scared and it something about which I do not really talking. But one day I was looking up the definition of what rolling in your own grave means. What it means is that somebody that who passed will be angry or upset about something. But were not perfect we still do that when we are alive. These things I do not really like talking about them. But it must be done. We all have different opinions and meanings. Like I said you must take the good with the bad. Just remember no one is perfect we all make mistakes. We all must learn from them even if it comes back to us and somedays you will think about it and not get it out of your head. Just remember that life goes on. Your loved ones will always be with you wherever you go.

Made in the USA
Monee, IL
10 December 2022

20780604R00046